EXPLORING CONTINENTS

EUROPE

Jane Bingham

Heinemann LIBRARY

www.heinemann.co.uk/library
Visit our website to find out more information about Heinemann Library books.

To order:
☎ Phone 44 (0) 1865 888066
📄 Send a fax to 44 (0) 1865 314091
💻 Visit the Heinemann Bookshop at www.heinemann.co.uk/library to browse our catalogue and order online.

First published in Great Britain by Heinemann, Halley Court, Jordan Hill, Oxford, OX2 8EJ, part of Harcourt Education.

Editorial: Louise Galpine and Harriet Milles
Design: Richard Parker and Q2A Solutions
Illustrations: Jeff Edwards
Picture Research: Mica Brancic and Beatrice Ray
Production: Camilla Crask

Originated by Chroma
Printed and bound in China by WKT

10 digit ISBN 0 431 09746 1 (hardback)
13 digit ISBN 978 0 431 09746 6 (hardback)

11 10 09 08 07
10 9 8 7 6 5 4 3 2 1

British Library Cataloguing in Publication Data
Bingham, Jane
  Europe. - (Exploring continents)
  1.Europe - Geography - Juvenile literature
  I.Title
  914
A full catalogue record for this book is available from the British Library.

Acknowledgements
Alamy pp. **8** (David Crossland), **15** (ImageState/ Mark Hamblin), **17** (Alex Segre), **20** (Allover), **21** (Stock Connection); Corbis pp. **9** (Michael Busselle), **22**; Getty pp. **5** (Taxi), **7** (Photodisc), **10** (Stone), **11** (Photographer's choice), **13** (StockImage), **14** (Image bank), **18** (Getty Entertainment), **23** (Lonely Planet), **24** (Getty News), **25** (Lonely Planet); Travel Ink p. **27**.

Cover satellite image of Europe reproduced with permission of SPL/Planetary Visions Ltd.

Every effort has been made to contact copyright holders of any material reproduced in this book. Any omissions will be rectified in subsequent printings if notice is given to the publishers.

CONTENTS

Words that appear in the text in bold, **like this**, are explained in the Glossary.

WHAT IS A CONTINENT?

A continent is a vast mass of land that covers part of the Earth's surface. There are seven continents in the world – Africa, Antarctica, Asia, Australia, Europe, North America, and South America.

Most of the world's continents contain several countries. Europe includes more than 40 countries, but it is still very small. Europe is the world's second smallest continent, after Australia.

Where is Europe?

The continent of Europe lies above the **equator** in the **northern hemisphere**. Parts of its northernmost countries lie inside the **Arctic Circle**.

This map shows the seven continents of the world.

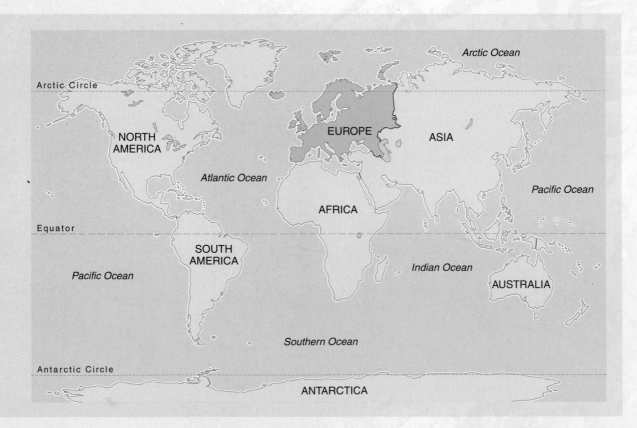

Arctic Ocean

Arctic Circle

NORTH AMERICA

EUROPE

ASIA

Atlantic Ocean

Pacific Ocean

AFRICA

Equator

SOUTH AMERICA

Pacific Ocean

Indian Ocean

AUSTRALIA

Southern Ocean

Antarctic Circle

ANTARCTICA

Europe is surrounded on three sides by water. To the north is the icy Arctic Ocean. To the west is the Atlantic Ocean and to the south is the Mediterranean Sea.

The warm Mediterranean Sea separates southern Europe from the continent of Africa.

To the east of Europe lies a vast area of land. This is the enormous continent of Asia. Two of Europe's countries belong to Asia as well. Russia and Turkey lie partly in Europe and partly in Asia.

Different regions

When people talk about Europe, they often divide it into regions. Western Europe includes the United Kingdom, France, Germany, Austria, Switzerland, and the Netherlands. Eastern Europe includes Poland, Romania, Hungary, and Russia. Southern Europe includes Portugal, Spain, Italy, Greece, and Turkey. The northern European countries of Denmark, Norway, Sweden, Finland, and Iceland all belong to Scandinavia.

Many islands

The continent of Europe contains many islands. Most of these islands are very small and belong to larger countries, but some are **independent** nations. The island of Iceland, in the far north of the Atlantic Ocean, is a country in its own right.

WHAT DOES EUROPE LOOK LIKE?

Mountain ranges

Northwest Europe is a region of mountains and deep valleys. This mountainous region includes Scandinavia and the northern half of the United Kingdom. In southern Europe, a series of mountain peaks stretch from east to west. These high southern ranges include the Alps and Pyrenees in Western Europe and the Carpathians in Eastern Europe.

In the northeast, the snow-capped Ural Mountains separate Europe from the continent of Asia. The Caucasus Mountains, in the southeast, also form a border with Asia. Mount Elbrus, in the Caucasus Mountains, is Europe's highest peak.

This map shows some of the dramatic natural features found in Europe.

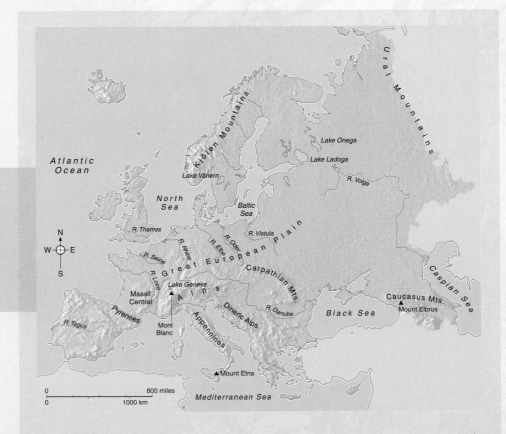

The Alps are more than 1200 km (750 miles) long and cross several countries, including France, Italy, Switzerland, Austria, Germany, and Serbia and Montenegro.

A great plain

In the centre of Europe is a wide, flat plain. This low-lying land has many rivers running through it, and it is mostly very good for farming. The Great European Plain stretches from northern France, through Belgium, the Netherlands, and Germany, into Eastern Europe.

Bays, inlets, and fjords

The coast of Europe has many natural bays and **inlets** which are often used as harbours for fishing boats. The long, narrow, steep-sided inlets along the coast of Norway are known as fjords (say fee-yords). Some of them are extremely deep and Sogn Fjord is 204 km (127 miles) long.

Did you know?

Southern Europe has several **active volcanoes** which still **erupt** occasionally. The biggest volcano in Europe is Mount Etna on the island of Sicily. The last time it erupted was in 2002.

Long rivers

Europe's longest river is the Volga, which flows through Russia.
It is frozen along most of its length for three months in winter.

In Western Europe, the River Rhine runs through the Netherlands,
Germany, and Switzerland. In 1992 a canal was completed in
Germany, which linked the Rhine to the River Danube. The
Danube flows east through Europe, crossing nine countries before
it reaches the Black Sea.

Ships and barges
can travel all the
way across Europe,
using the Rhine
(pictured left) and
Danube rivers.

Europe's lakes

Europe has many large **freshwater** lakes. The largest is Lake
Ladoga in Russia. Lake Ladoga used to be filled with fish. Now
many of these fish are dying because the lake is polluted. Some
lakes and rivers in Europe have been polluted by chemical waste
from factories or by **pesticides** from farms.

Switzerland is famous for its lakes and mountains. People go sailing and windsurfing on these lakes as well as enjoying the tranquil scenery.

Switzerland has many beautiful lakes, such as Lake Lucerne and Lake Geneva. Some lakes in Europe provide water for people to use in their homes. Water from these lakes is given a special treatment to make it safe to drink.

Sea or lake?

The Caspian Sea in Eastern Europe is really a lake, because it is entirely surrounded by land. However, it is filled with salt water like a sea. Experts believe that the Caspian Sea was originally joined to a larger ocean. Then, around 11 million years ago, it became cut off from the ocean. The Caspian Sea is the largest area of inland water in the world. It is larger than the country of Japan in Asia.

WHAT IS THE WEATHER LIKE IN EUROPE?

The weather in Europe varies greatly. In the south of the continent, the **climate** is warm and sunny. In the far north, it is freezing cold. In large areas of northern Europe, the weather is wet and mild.

The icy north

The countries of Scandinavia and northern Russia have a very cold, snowy climate. In the summer, the snow melts but the weather is still cool. Inside the Arctic Circle, temperatures in winter are often as low as minus 60°C (minus 140°F).

The northernmost part of Europe, within the Arctic Circle, is known as the Land of the Midnight Sun. This is because, in June and July, the sun does not set and there is constant daylight for 60 days. In December and January, the opposite happens – the sun does not rise and there are 60 days of darkness.

During the winter months, countries like Iceland are covered with snow and very few plants can grow.

The sunny Greek islands are busy in the summer with tourists who come to enjoy their warm weather.

The warm south

The countries beside the Mediterranean Sea have hot, sunny summers and mild winters. This gentle climate makes southern Europe a very popular place for holidaymakers. The Mediterranean climate is also ideal for growing olives and grapes.

Wet and mild

Countries in Western Europe have a mild, **temperate** climate, with lots of rain and mist. These countries do not get very cold in winter or very hot in summer. Warm **currents** from the Atlantic Ocean stop the coasts of Western Europe from becoming icy. However, in Eastern Europe, the winters are much colder. In most parts of Europe, the high **mountain ranges** are covered with snow during the winter months.

Did you know?

European weather facts

Highest recorded temperature: Seville, Spain: 50°C (122°F)

Lowest recorded temperature: Ust'Shchugor, Russia: minus 67°C (minus 89°F)

WHAT PLANTS AND ANIMALS LIVE IN EUROPE?

Cold weather plants

In the frozen north, only a few plants can survive. Inside the Arctic Circle, there is a type of landscape called **tundra**. Plants that grow on the tundra are mainly mosses and **lichens**, but a few bushes and small trees can also grow in the thin soil.

Below the Arctic Circle, there are vast forests of firs, pines, and other evergreen trees. Trees that keep their leaves in winter are known as coniferous trees. The people of Scandinavia and northern Russia cut down these trees and use their wood. Sometimes they plant new trees to replace the ones they have cut down.

Many types of plants live in the different climates of Europe.

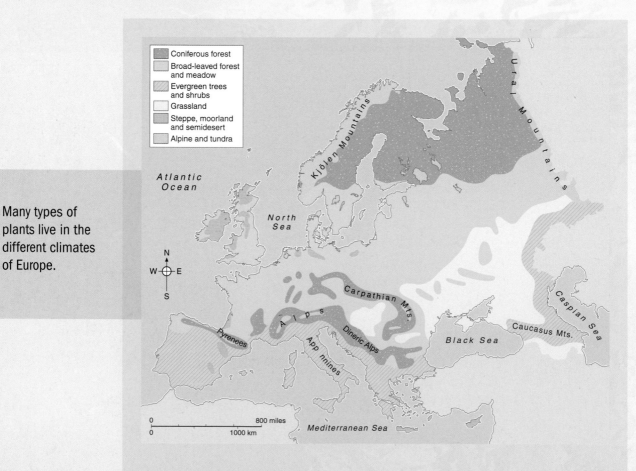

Coniferous forest
Broad-leaved forest and meadow
Evergreen trees and shrubs
Grassland
Steppe, moorland and semidesert
Alpine and tundra

Atlantic Ocean

Kjølen Mountains

Ural Mountains

North Sea

N
W · E
S

Carpathian Mts.

Alps

Pyrenees

Apennines

Dineric Alps

Black Sea

Caucasus Mts.

Caspian Sea

0   800 miles
0   1000 km

Mediterranean Sea

Mild weather plants

In Western and central Europe, there are forests of deciduous trees (trees that lose their leaves in winter). Oaks, beeches, and sycamore trees are all examples of deciduous trees. The mild, wet climate of Western Europe is also good for growing flowers. In the Netherlands, farmers grow tulips and sell them all over the world.

Warm weather plants

In the warm south of Europe, farmers grow orange and lemon trees, olive trees and grapes. Grapes are planted in vineyards and crushed to make into wine. Olives are crushed to make olive oil.

All over Europe, wild flowers grow in forests and meadows. In the mountains of Switzerland, delicate **alpine flowers** emerge every springtime.

Did you know?

In Eastern Europe and Russia there are vast stretches of flat, empty land, known as the steppes. Here, short, springy grasses are the main form of **vegetation**. Very few trees grow on the steppes because it is too cold and windy.

Wild animals

Five hundred years ago, there were wild bears and wolves all over Europe. Now most of them have been hunted and shot. However, some bears and wolves still survive in isolated areas. There are also plenty of wild deer, badgers, and foxes living in Europe.

Inside the Arctic Circle, polar bears and seals live on the ice. Meanwhile, the warm climate of southern Europe is perfect for lizards and snakes.

In the far north of the continent, herds of reindeer roam the snowy wastes of Russia and Scandinavia.

Did you know?

Some creatures living inside the Arctic Circle have different summer and winter coats. In winter, the Arctic fox and snowshoe hare have white coats so that they do not stand out against the snow. In summer, when the snow melts, their coats turn brown so that they blend in easily with the rocks and plants.

Birds of Europe

Europe has a wide range of birds. In the hills and mountains are eagles and **buzzards**. Elegant white swans glide on Europe's rivers, and brilliant turquoise kingfishers can sometimes be spotted darting over the water. Europe's forests are home to owls and woodpeckers.

Many birds spend the summer in Europe but then **migrate** to warmer parts of the world. Swallows, geese, and swans migrate to Africa each autumn and return to Europe in the spring as the weather becomes warmer.

Water wildlife

Europe's lakes, ponds, and rivers are home to an amazing range of fish and other creatures. In the rivers of northern Europe, there are wild salmon and trout. Frogs and newts live in Europe's rivers and ponds, while mayflies and dragonflies hover on the water's surface.

Otters (pictured left) and water rats make their homes in the banks of Europe's rivers.

WHAT ARE EUROPE'S NATURAL RESOURCES?

People in Europe produce and sell a wide range of products. In many parts of Europe, farming is the main way of earning money. Fishing is also important for many countries. Europe has many factories and mines, but it also has some exciting new **industries.**

Farming in Europe

All over Europe, farmers grow wheat that is ground into flour. The flour is used mainly for making bread. In southern Europe, wheat traditionally is made into bread and pasta. Other important crops are barley, rye, and oats.

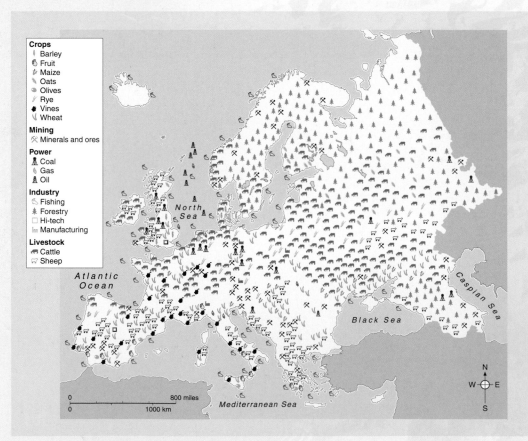

Crops
- Barley
- Fruit
- Maize
- Oats
- Olives
- Rye
- Vines
- Wheat

Mining
- Minerals and ores

Power
- Coal
- Gas
- Oil

Industry
- Fishing
- Forestry
- Hi-tech
- Manufacturing

Livestock
- Cattle
- Sheep

North Sea

Atlantic Ocean

Caspian Sea

Black Sea

0   800 miles
0   1000 km

Mediterranean Sea

N W E S

This map shows some of the natural resources and industries in Europe.

Northern Europe has many dairy farms, where cows are kept for their milk. The milk is then made into cream, butter, yoghurt, and cheese. The dairy farmers of the Netherlands and France are especially famous for their cheeses.

Many farmers in Europe breed cows, sheep, and pigs for their meat. Scottish beef, Welsh lamb, and Danish bacon are **exported** to countries all over the world.

In the warm, dry countries around the Mediterranean Sea, farmers mainly grow fruit, olives, and grapes. Spain is famous for its oranges, while Greece and Italy produce fine olive oil. France, Spain, Italy, and Germany all make excellent wines that are sold around the world.

Some fishermen in Europe still use small boats (below). However, most fishing today is done by huge trawlers that drag enormous nets behind them.

The fishing industry

All round the coast of Europe, people catch fish. In the cold northern seas they catch cod, herring, and haddock. **Squid** and octopus are caught off the southern coasts of Italy and Spain.

Did you know?

Fish in danger

Large fishing trawlers can catch thousands of fish on each trip. This means that there are not enough fish left to breed in the sea, and some types of fish are in danger of dying out. In order to protect the fish, European countries have made strict laws for trawlers.

Timber, mining, and drilling

Scandinavia and Russia both have major timber industries. Timber from their huge forests is used to make furniture, cardboard, and paper. It is also used to heat people's homes.

Many parts of Europe are rich in coal, oil, and other **minerals**. In Russia, Scandinavia, and Eastern Europe, people drill for oil and **mine** for coal, iron, and precious metals. There are also good supplies of **natural gas** under the North Sea.

Europe's factories

Germany, France, Italy, and the Czech Republic all have large car factories. Many factories in Eastern Europe produce steel and large machinery. In Western Europe, most factories produce smaller goods, such as mobile phones and computer parts.

Other industries

Large numbers of people work in Europe's tourist and travel industry. Some work in restaurants, shops, and hotels. Others look after people on their holidays.

All over Europe, a growing number of people work in the computer industry. Many of them design **computer software**.

Europe leads the world in fashion design. Milan, Paris, and London are all major fashion centres, where clothes are designed and made.

WHAT COUNTRIES AND CITIES ARE IN EUROPE?

Europe is made up of 47 countries. These countries vary greatly in size. Russia is by far the largest country in Europe. The part of Russia that lies in Europe measures about 4,526,000 square kilometres (1,747,112 square miles). The Vatican City is Europe's smallest country. It contains the **Pope's** palace and it measures less than a quarter of a mile square (just over half a square kilometre).

How are Europe's countries run?

Each country in Europe has its own government. These governments make decisions about how their country is run. Most countries in Europe have a **president**, but a few countries have a monarch (a king or a queen). The United Kingdom, Spain, and Belgium are all countries with a monarch.

This map shows the countries and major cities of Europe.

The European Union

Some countries in Europe have joined a group called the European Union. This is also known as the EU. Members of the EU meet to discuss how they can work together and help each other. The EU members meet at the European **Parliament**. This is held in Strasbourg (in France) and Brussels (in Belgium). Most EU countries use the same money – Euro bank notes and coins.

Capital cities

Each country has a capital city, usually where the country's government meets. These cities contain many beautiful buildings. Paris, the capital of France, is one of the world's most elegant cities. It has wide tree-lined streets and many parks.

The new European Parliament building at Strasbourg. The colourful national flags illustrate that the EU brings together many European nations.

Did you know?

Watery capital
Sweden's capital, Stockholm, is built on 14 islands.
The islands are linked to each other by many bridges.

Russians call this square *Krasnaya ploshchad*. *Krasnaya* can mean either "red" or "beautiful" in Russian, which is why it is called Red Square in English.

The capital of Russia is Moscow. At its centre is a walled area, called the Kremlin. This is where the Russian government meets. Next to the Kremlin is Red Square, which contains the famous St. Basil's Cathedral.

The city of Rome is Italy's capital. It was also the centre of the great Roman Empire, two thousand years ago. Today, Rome has a mixture of ancient ruins and modern buildings.

The Berlin Wall separated East and West Germany. The wall ran through the middle of Berlin, past the Brandenburg Gate. It was taken down in 1989.

Europe divided

For more than 40 years after the Second World War, Europe was divided into two halves. The countries in Eastern Europe had **communist** governments. These governments owned all their country's land and controlled all their people's jobs. People in Eastern Europe were not allowed to leave their countries.

While Eastern Europe was ruled by communists, the countries of Western Europe had **democratic** governments. These governments were chosen by their people, who voted for them in **elections**. People in Western Europe had much more freedom than people in Eastern Europe.

Europe reunited

From 1989, the countries of Eastern Europe stopped being communist. They set up democratic governments and Europe was united again. Now people can travel wherever they want to in Europe.

WHO LIVES IN EUROPE?

Europe has an amazing range of different **nationalities.** The people in Europe belong to 47 different countries. Many live in their own countries, but some travel to other parts of Europe to study or work. Europe is also home to many **immigrants** – people from foreign countries who have settled in Europe and made it their home.

Many languages

Most countries in Europe have their own language, and some countries have more than one language. As well as speaking their own language, many people in Europe also speak English. This helps them to communicate with each other.

Newspaper stands in Belgium often carry papers in Walloon and Flemish as both languages are widely spoken in the country.

Did you know?

The small country of Belgium has three **official languages**.
• People in northern Belgium speak Walloon (a version of French).
• People in southern Belgium speak Flemish (a version of Dutch).
• A small number of people in eastern Belgium speak German.
One tenth of Belgium's population are immigrants. These people mainly speak their **native languages** – Italian, Spanish, Greek, Arabic, or Turkish.

Some people come to Europe for a short time – either to study or to work. Many people come to live in Europe permanently.

A varied society

Europe today is home to people from all over the world. Even though these **immigrants** were born in a different continent, most of them soon see themselves as Europeans.

Different lives

People in Europe have many different ways of life. Often, Europeans live in large, bustling cities. They travel to work by underground, bus, or train. Europe's city centres are filled with tall office blocks and shops where people work.

Other people in Europe live more **traditional** lives in the countryside. They work on the land and live in small villages or farmhouses. In remote parts of Eastern Europe and Russia, life in the countryside has changed very little in hundreds of years.

In some parts of Europe, people still keep up their ancient traditions. In Scotland, men dressed in kilts play the bagpipes and dance highland jigs. In Spain, people go to bullfights, where they watch **matadors** try to dodge charging bulls.

In Krakow, Poland, folk dancers gather to perform in traditional costumes to celebrate special occasions or holidays.

Different religions

The main religion in Europe is Christianity. Europe has many beautiful churches and cathedrals that were built over a thousand years ago.

In Turkey and parts of Eastern Europe, most people are Muslims. Europe is also home to many Jewish people. As well as these main religions, some immigrants from other countries have brought their own religions to Europe.

25

WHAT FAMOUS PLACES ARE IN EUROPE?

The continent of Europe has many natural wonders. It also has a long and fascinating history. People come from all over the world to see Europe's ancient buildings and its spectacular sights.

Natural wonders

Tourists travel to Switzerland to see its beautiful mountains and lakes. They take boat trips down Norway's rocky fjords, and they visit Iceland to see the **geysers** spouting hot steam. In southern Europe, the Greek islands have white, sandy beaches and brilliant blue seas.

This map shows some of the amazing wonders that can be found across Europe.

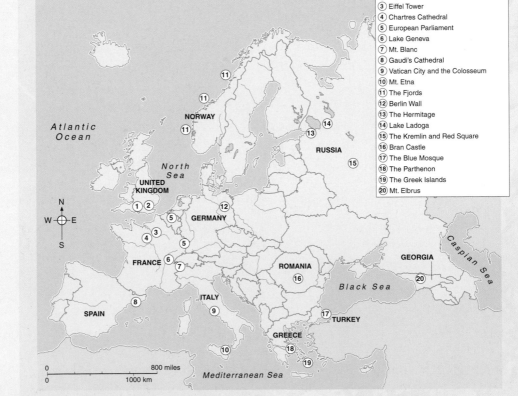

1. Stonehenge
2. Big Ben and the Houses of Parliament
3. Eiffel Tower
4. Chartres Cathedral
5. European Parliament
6. Lake Geneva
7. Mt. Blanc
8. Gaudi's Cathedral
9. Vatican City and the Colosseum
10. Mt. Etna
11. The Fjords
12. Berlin Wall
13. The Hermitage
14. Lake Ladoga
15. The Kremlin and Red Square
16. Bran Castle
17. The Blue Mosque
18. The Parthenon
19. The Greek Islands
20. Mt. Elbrus

Tourists flock to London to see Big Ben and the Houses of Parliament.

City sights

The cities of Europe are filled with famous monuments and buildings. In Paris, tourists visit the Eiffel Tower. In Istanbul, they marvel at the Blue Mosque.

Castles, palaces, and cathedrals

Europe has many castles, dating from the Middle Ages (about 1000–1450 AD). One of the most dramatic is Bran Castle in Romania. The Hermitage Palace in St Petersburg, Russia, was once the home of the Russian royal family. Now it is the world's largest art gallery. The Italian city of Venice is filled with medieval palaces, on the banks of the city's canals.

In cities all over Europe, there are massive cathedrals, with soaring spires. Chartres Cathedral in France is famous for its stained glass windows. The Spanish city of Barcelona has a very unusual cathedral designed by the architect, Antonio Gaudi. It is still being built.

Ancient history

The cities of Athens and Rome are scattered with ruined temples and palaces from the time of the Ancient Greeks and Romans. In Athens, a vast temple known as the Parthenon stands on a hill above the city. The Colosseum in Rome is a giant stone stadium. In Roman times it was used for **gladiator** fights.

27

CONTINENTS COMPARISON CHART

Continent	Area	Population	
AFRICA	30,365,000 square kilometres (11,720,000 square miles)	906 million	
ANTARCTICA	14,200,000 square kilometres (5,500,000 square miles)	officially none, but about 4,000 people live on the research stations during the summer and over 3,000 people visit as tourists each year. People have lived there for as long as three and a half years at a time.	
ASIA	44,614,000 square kilometres (17,226,200 square miles)	almost 4,000 million	
AUSTRALIA	7,713,364 square kilometres (2,966,136 square miles)	approximately 20,090,400 (2005 estimate)	
EUROPE	10,400,000 square kilometres (4,000,000 square miles)	approximately 727 million (2005 estimate)	
NORTH AMERICA	24,230,000 square kilometres (9,355,000 square miles)	approximately 509,915,000 (2005 estimate)	
SOUTH AMERICA	17,814,000 square kilometres (6,878,000 square miles)	380 million	

Number of Countries	Highest Point	Longest River
54 (includes Western Sahara)	Mount Kilimanjaro, Tanzania — 5,895 metres (19,340 feet)	Nile River — 6,695 kilometres (4,160 miles)
none, but over 23 countries have research stations in Antarctica	Vinson Massif — 4,897 metres (16,067 feet)	River Onyx — 12 kilometres (7.5 miles) **Biggest Ice Shelf** Ross Ice Shelf in western Antarctica — 965 kilometres (600 miles) long.
50	Mount Everest, Tibet and Nepal — 8,850 metres (29,035 feet)	Yangtze River, China — 6,300 kilometres (3,914 miles)
1	Mount Kosciusko — 2,229 metres (7,313 fcct)	Murray River — 2,520 kilometres (1,566 miles)
47	Mount Elbrus, Russia — 5,642 metres (18,510 feet)	River Volga — 3,685 kilometres (2,290 miles)
23	Mount McKinley (Denali) in Alaska — 6,194 metres (20,320 feet)	Mississippi/Missouri River System — 6,270 kilometres (3,895 miles)
12	Aconcagua, Argentina — 6,959 metres (22,834 feet)	Amazon River — 6,400 kilometres (4,000 miles)

GLOSSARY

active volcano mountain that erupts from time to time, throwing out ash and hot rocks from a large hole in its top

alpine flower flower that grows on mountains

Arctic Circle imaginary line that runs around the top part of the globe. Above the Arctic Circle is the Arctic, an area of ice and snow around the North Pole.

buzzard large bird of prey that looks rather like an eagle

capital city city where a country's government is based

climate kind of weather that an area has

communist way of running a country, in which all the land, houses, and factories belong to the government

computer software general name for the programs used in a computer to make it do different jobs

current movement of water in a sea or a river

democratic way of running a country in which all the people have the right to vote in elections for their leaders

election time when people vote for someone or something

equator imaginary line running around the middle of the Earth

erupt to throw out ash and hot rocks

exported sent abroad to be sold

freshwater water that does not contain salt

geyser hole in the ground through which hot water and steam shoot up in bursts

gladiator ancient Roman warrior who fought against other gladiators and wild animals

immigrant someone who comes from abroad to live permanently in a country

independent free from control by another country

industry business of making things, which are sold to make money

inlet long, narrow channel, where a river flows into the sea

lichen flat, moss-like plant that grows on rocks and trees

matador bull fighter

migrate to travel to a different region at a particular time of year

mine to dig up minerals from under the ground

mineral natural substance found in the Earth, such as diamond or gold

mountain range lots of mountains in a row

nationality country to which a person belongs

native language language that a person has learned to speak in his or her own country

natural gas gas that is found underground

northern hemisphere all the land that lies above the equator, in the northern half of the globe

official language language that is used for government and business

parliament group of people who make the laws of a country

pesticide spray used to kill pests, especially insects

Pope head of the Roman Catholic Church

president head of a country, who has been chosen in an election

squid sea creature with a long, soft body and ten tentacles (or arms)

temperate moderate, not extreme

traditional done in the same way for hundreds of years

trawler fishing boat that drags a large, bag-shaped net through the water

tundra very cold areas, where the soil under the surface is always frozen

vegetation plants, bushes, and trees

FURTHER INFORMATION

Books

An Illustrated Atlas of Europe, Keith Lye (Cherrytree Books, 2000)
Continents: Europe, Leila Merrell Foster (Heinemann Library, 2002)
Europe, Ewan McLeish (Hodder Children's Books, 2000)
The World's Continents: Europe, Polly Goodman (Hodder Wayland, 2000)

Useful websites

* Find out about different cultures all over Europe:
  http://www.european-schoolprojects.net/festivals/
* Discover places of interest in different countries across Europe:
  http://www.geographia.com/indx03.htm
* Learn about the main European rivers:
  http://www.public.asu.edu/~goutam/gcu325/
* Find out more about the EU and the Euro:
  http://library.thinkquest.org/CR0215505/home.htm

Disclaimer

All the internet addresses (URLs) given in this book were valid at the time of going to press. However, due to the dynamic nature of the internet, some addresses may have changed, or sites may have ceased to exist since publication. While the author and publishers regret any inconvenience this may cause readers, no responsibility for such changes can be accepted by either the author(s) or the publishers.

Titles in the Exploring Continents series include:

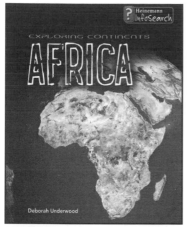

Deborah Underwood

Hardback   0 431 09742 9

Tristan Boyer Binns

Hardback   0 431 09743 7

Anita Ganeri

Hardback   0 431 09744 5

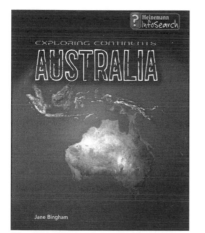

Jane Bingham

Hardback   0 431 09745 3

Jane Bingham

Hardback   0 431 09746 1

Tristan Boyer Binns

Hardback   0 431 09747 X

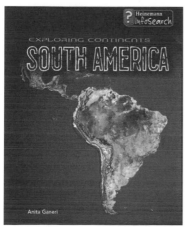

Anita Ganeri

Hardback   0 431 09748 8

Find out about other titles from Heinemann Library on our website www.heinemann.co.uk/library